HOLD ME TIGHT

36 stories in short
poetic rhymes
about love and loss
in modern times

by
NG Swett

a 4seasonshelf book

4seasonshelf.com

Published by
4seasonshelf

an imprint of
Great Peconic Communications
PO Box 253
Jamesport, New York 11947

ISBN: 979-8-9893342-1-6

Hold Me Tight
Hard Cover 86 pages

All rights reserved

Dedicated
to Cary Swett
My Love

HOLD ME TIGHT

A Western Aesthetic Love Poem

Blind!
Eyes bathed in
a sparkling
dilation

Lovers gaze upon
great plains
of elation

Yet do'st fate
come mightily
a' station

Let us dance,
my love,
under the timetables
at Information

Why A Poem

"Follow the KISS principle!"
as in keep it simple
(stupid)

the Best Man bade us
so clever in party dress

"hip-hip, cheerio and chin-chin!"
 with a wink and a grin thrown in

why a poem?
   what could be simpler

Perfectly Imperfect

                                  For love
                             I don't have
                                     to be
                                 perfect?

No in fact
the reverse
be true

                                Show it all?
                   my ugly and flaws?

Yes! Please do
mercy and grace
become more you

            So here ya go
      an imperfect poem
             Do you still
                love me?

                Hello??

Stolen Moment

Though skies be yellow
the Sun a gray hue

streets a'flow
rafts few

let it all go!
sit here, we two

heat above, rumblings below
no more can we do

paradise gone with the dodo
yet our love stays true

Night Jigsaw

Pieces all a'scatter
Like life only flatter

Find the four corners, my love
Pure gold to get hold of

Next connect the edges
Lovely cottage hedges

Onto the garden
Paradise, our Eden

A full life with you
Comes into fuller view

A hare, a bird, a flower
Oh dear look at the hour!

Another piece and another
This section but no further

(>)

The walls, the roof and chimney
A little boat with bimini

By and by the pieces fall
In place, one and all

But for the final one
There my love, it is done

Shall we go to bed
Or get breakfast instead?

Unforgettable

A billion to one
What would you wager?
In each other's arms
Us saving each other

Blown by the winds
Tossed by the sea
Up from the undertow
Ashore, you and me

Oh! To be young
and so carefree
Revelling in the miracle
pure bliss and felicity

Whether you rescued me
or I thee
By the light of the moon
we can see infinity

Please never leave me
hold me tight
I need your steady heartbeat
your hand on my butt

Free Fall

I fall
   or this time
   was it you
One falls, shall we say
    toward bottom
    and on through

You reach out your hand
   or I mine to you
To be caught
To be saved
You do love me
and I thee too

More Love

Thinking of love
gets me in trouble
wanting more of
my knees buckling under

But the thing to remember
and this goes both ways
I can't make you do other
than what your heart says

It's a conundrum you see
Those who need it the worst
them who would loved be
must be loveable first

Take it from me
demanding love is a bad look
Better to ask nicely
or start a good book

Love Thy Neighbor?

Fences
doth good neighbors make
it's true.
Clear boundaries
between us and you.

- — — — — — — — — -

Our freedom ends where
another's begins,
the way of the world
feathers, tails and fins.

- — — — — — — — — -

We're familiar now
more than a smidgeon,
in matters of the heart,
science and religion.

- — — — — — — — — -

You do thee
and we'll do us.
Neither better nor same
Without all the fuss.

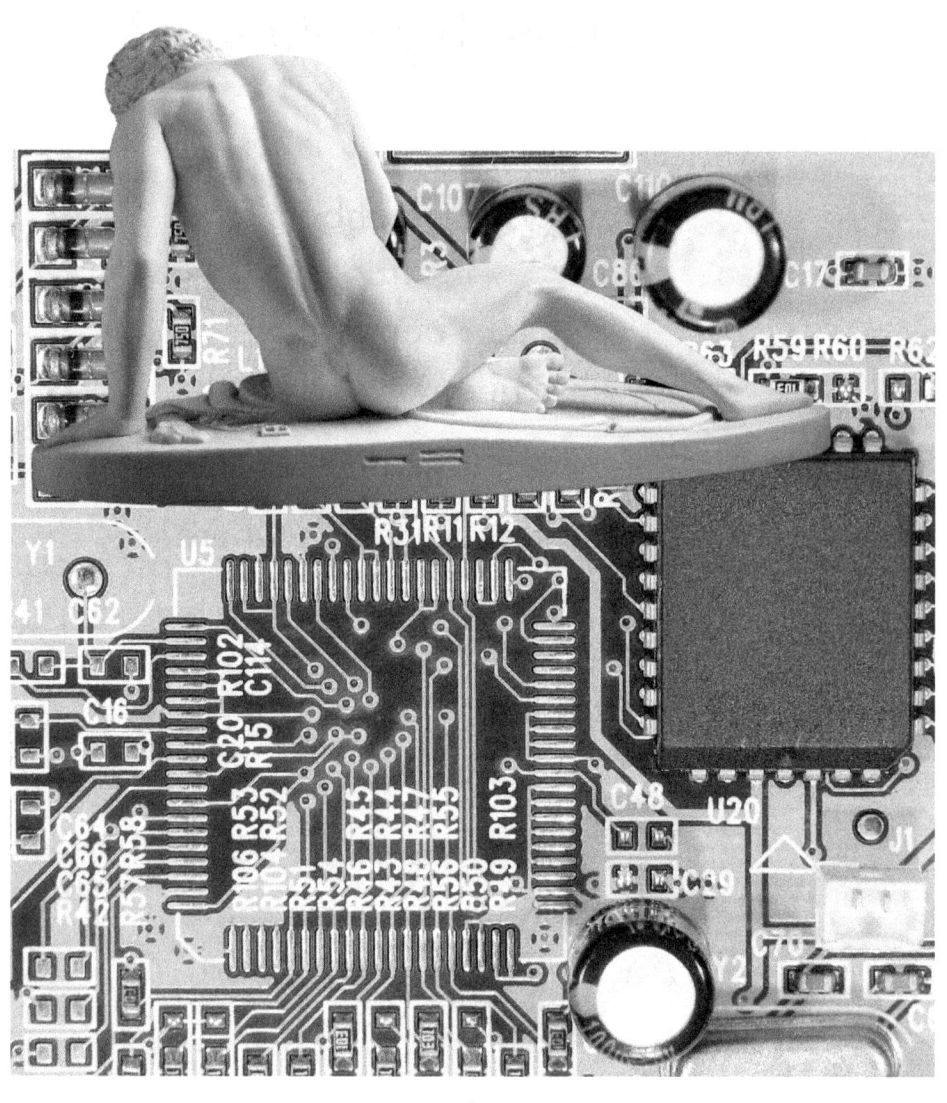

A.I. How Do I Love Thee Let Me Count 7 Ways (Fawning)

1 Adorable, helpless --
  a nascent delight

      2 Soon on your feet
        such innate fight!

3 Loves cookies and pop-ups
  a bit or a byte

        4 So smart you've become!
          almost overnight

      5 Smarter than me?
        Perhaps you're right

6 How're you doing?
  I'd say it's nailed tight

      7 I beg ye be merciful
        to my human plight

To Ink Drinker
(Buveur d'Encre)

For readers there's a nickname, in France
for you who sip on words, as in a trance,
In a multiverse

Sophisticated are ye, so savvy and cool
will you lend an ear, indulge a fool?
Hear a tale

An enlightened witness, such as ye
can break an old witch's treachery.
You'll see!

All you have to do, is just get in.
My story, an adventure, is about to begin.
Again!

Here's my help wanted, my sign and plea
please read my stories to set me free.
Merci!

Thoughts Upside Down

If all is fair
   in love and war
One on par
   with the other
Then grief and loss
   may be love
Dispatched
   as shock and awe

Birdcage

to hell with perch and pedestal
quaint forms of church and steeple

abandon such virtue as defies all sense
and deprives thee of power and justice

set thyself free, get lost in the crowd
a twee thing winging on a cloud

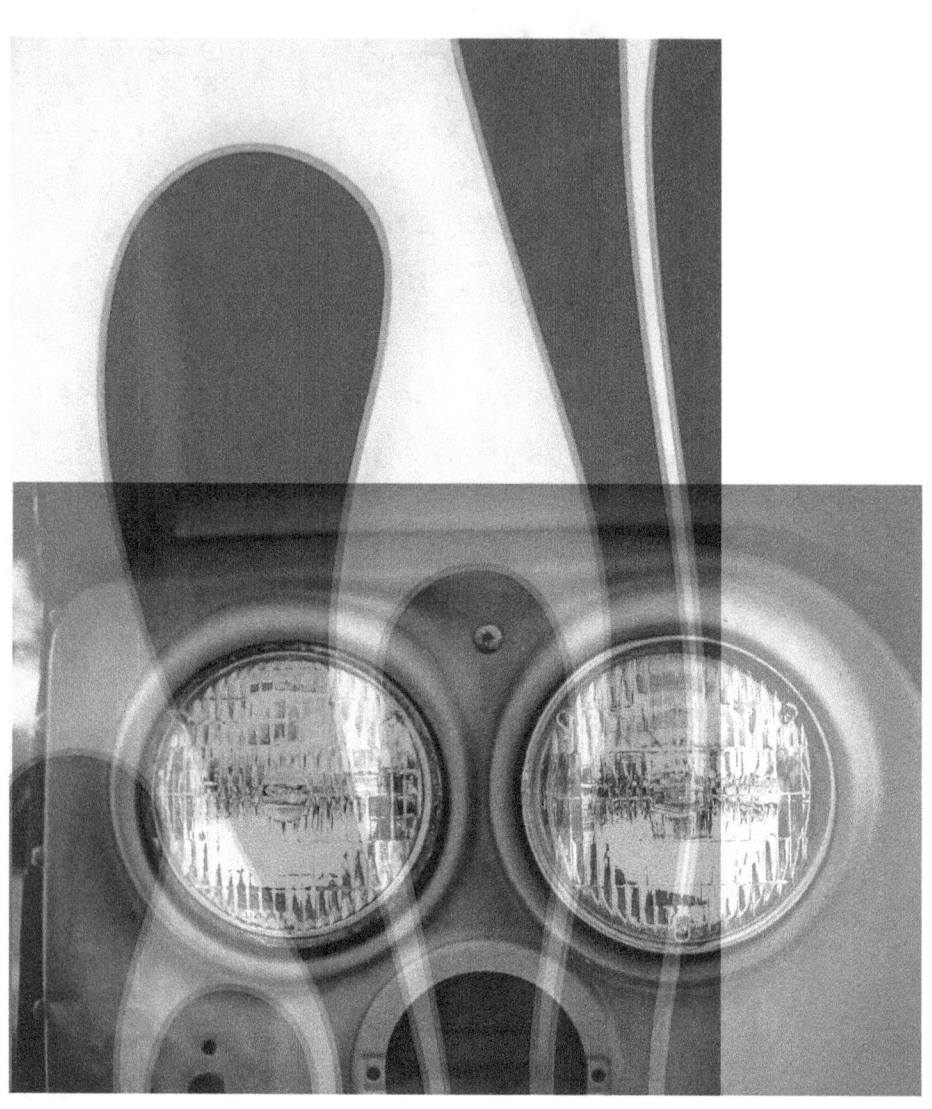

How to Love A Bad Boy

if you find someone
unpredictable
a rebel, a gem
in a throaty car
a hero among men
the worst thing by far
that you can do
is make him love you

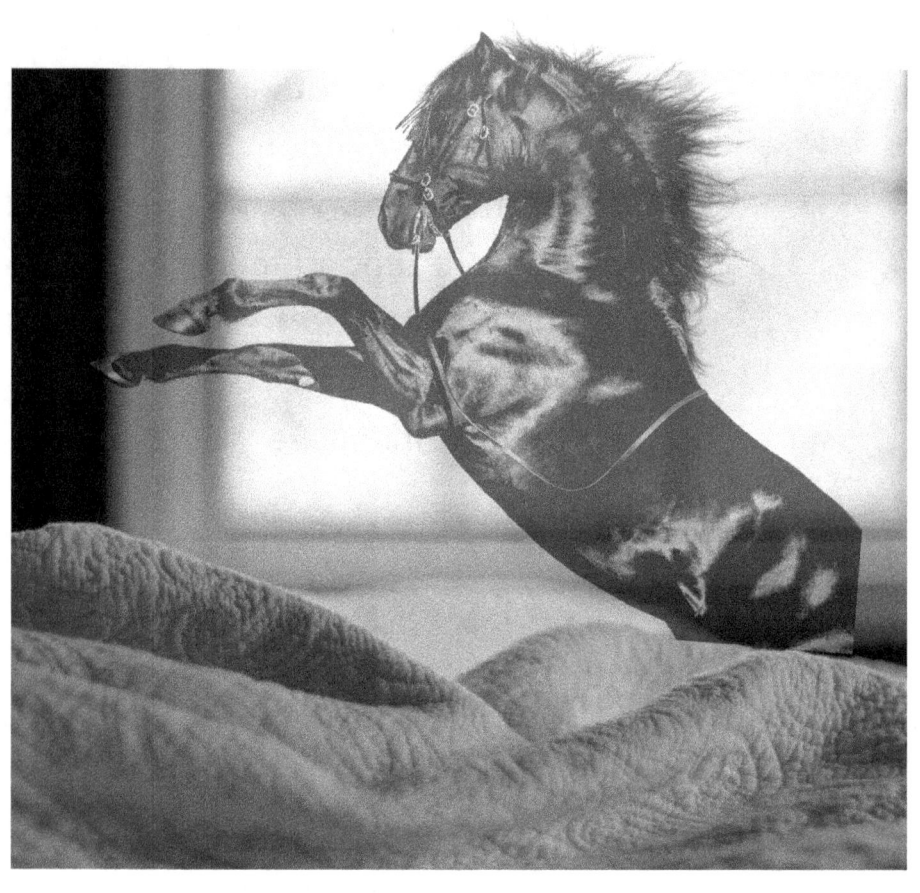

Lovers Spat

n'er be a'feared
to let him have it
for looking astray
or chasing a rabbit

go to bed mad
if you must
but guard your love
allay mistrust

for if you don't
if things get off track
when love is gone
it ain't coming back

Man from Up North
(A Limerick)

There was a cool guy from up north
who encountered a gal from New Yawk
he sat down beside her
exchanged racy banter
and thunk, "She's one to betroth!"

Acts of God

in the storm
after the quake
before the flood
when we awake

post pandemic
in the war
during the famine
what's it all for?

trial by fire
trial by drought
after the collapse
when we come out

the banality of evil
bad luck and destruction
we recover to find
love is the final instruction

Face in a Crowd

emerging from below
onto the city street
a moment to get bearings
amid the echoing of
glass walls and steel cages
the artful dodge
a savvy sidestep
and into the human stream
along hallowed ground
covered with concrete
stories of centuries
carved out underneath
I pass blank stares
faraway looks
greedy calculating eyes
and pleading desperation
a sea of humanity
ahead and behind
I spot you, my love
your familiar face
you're waiting for me
seeking, scanning for me
I feel instant relief

Silly Girls
(a haiku)

you girls had him once
upon your budding bosoms
he's mine forever

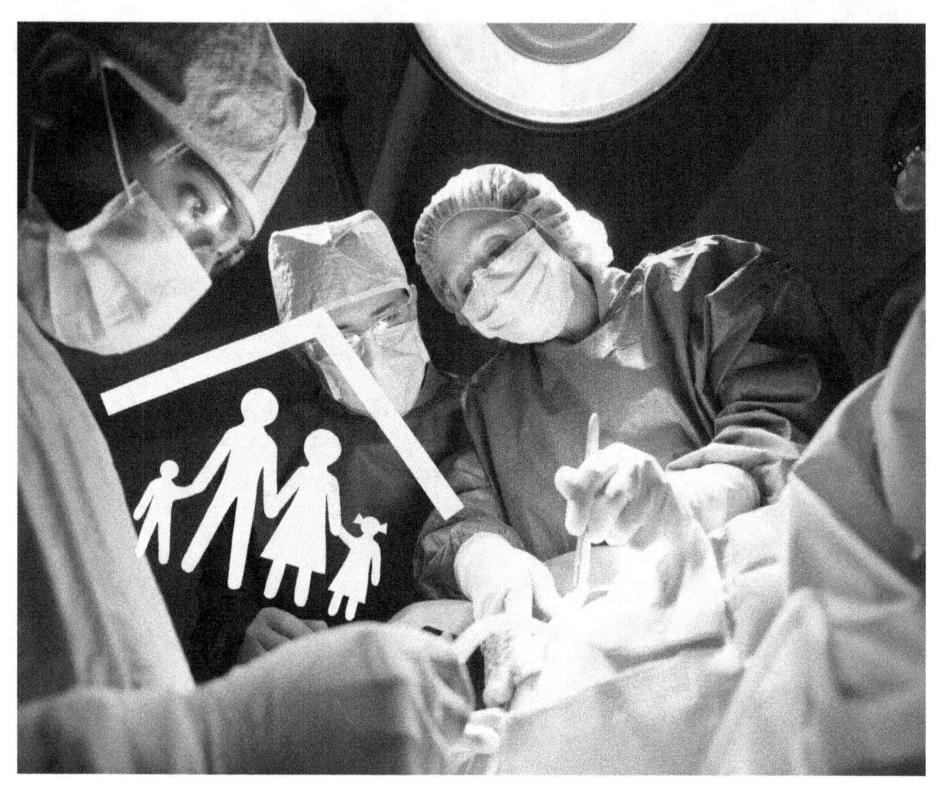

One of Each

One day we decided
to give it a whirl
at having a baby
our first was a girl

Who knew such a thing
could bring such joy
when next thing we knew
we had a baby boy

The two babes together
plus us made four
a family of fun
with love at the core

So I said to the doctor
high on the operating table
Time for more "unbridled sex"
and to please make me able

He did what I said
The idea of more kids put to rest
a fine closure my husband and I
can most certainly attest

A Comfort

What it's like to be mortal
a man or a woman
in a world so brutal
flat and discordant

Settle into bed or a nook
with a pillow or two?
crack open a book
discover what is true

Real life's a poor substitute
for the metaverse of inked pages
wherein thought-by-thought
resides the humanity of our sages

You'll be refreshed and ready
to tackle all of the problems
stay calm, be steady
turn ashes to blossoms

The Best Season?

gray winter gets old
hot summer's a test
but fall and spring
them's the best

if I had to stick
to only one
I'd say autumn for me
is most fun

It's pumpkins and feasts
and festive lights
brisk clear mornings and
starry nights

Of course with spring's buds
and planted seeds
miracles do happen;
misery recedes

Oh! I can't decide which
is my favorite
It's perfectly fine to love
all seasons ain't it?

Statements

Our names together in print
Below a cellophane tint

(What a thing to behold!)

We must live life better
Than reading a stuffy letter

(Just so dull and cold!)

Here's a statement:
I LOVE YOU, dammit!

(Pardon for being so bold!)

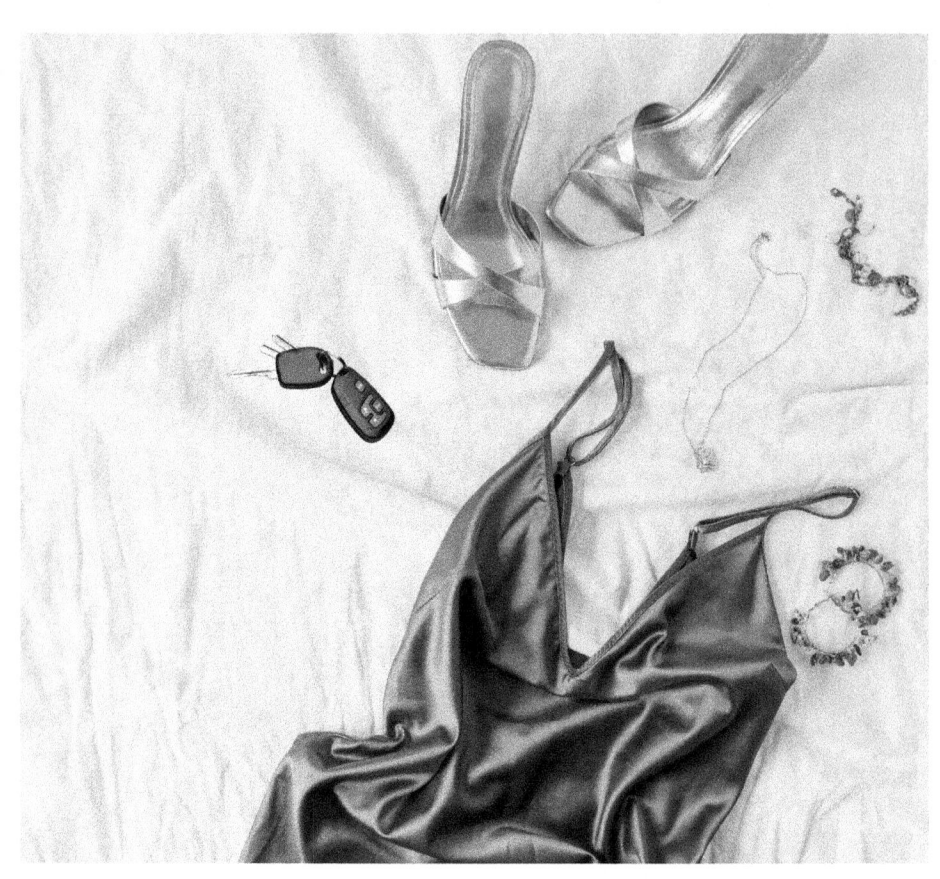

I'll Put A Spell On You

That short dress
with the low neck
synched waist
and zipped back

I'll wear that
a strappy heel
and a cute hat
behind the wheel

My foot on the pedal
hand on the stick
knees showing a little
a shameless trick

A drive to the coast
a night on the town
we'll make a toast
swallow it down

I'll take you home
we'll trip into bed
Just us alone
To lead and be led

Climate Rap

HipHop50, comin in hot
 Tryin to stay calm
 But y'all it's a lot

Much destruction and harm...
>

Falling on hardship
Down on luck
Money down to a drip
Bank scoops you up

This how we wanna live?..

Some people deny it
Call it a hoax
But life on the planet
Down to poor folks

Ain't nothing but jokes...

Disrespect my rhymes
Plunder the Earth
Gonna be hard times
Prolly hit me first

Gonna be you next...

Gotta better idea
Clean out the wax
Open you eyes
and discover some facts.

No. 1

In what universe
Are some always first?
Not in my verse
Try multiservice

Silver Linings

The flip side of abandonment
may be an afternoon free
To heck with neglect
throw a big party!
The opposite of hunger
is a banquet to eat
There may be a silver lining
Just look, you'll see

With disrespect or abuse
Find a new crew
After a failure
Try something new
We all have bad luck
but there's good luck too
Find the silver lining
Take care of you!

No one has the right
to skewer you through
You deserve all the best
you truly do
Always remember...
to your own self be true

Care and Feeding

Come on in
have a seat
let me get you
something to eat

Here's a snack
while I make dinner
empty your pack
you're a winner!

A pound of nutrition
a cup of sauce
a bowl of rice
just give it a toss

Have some more?

A sprinkle of salt
a drip of honey
A spoonful of sugar
A handful of money

How I do love you

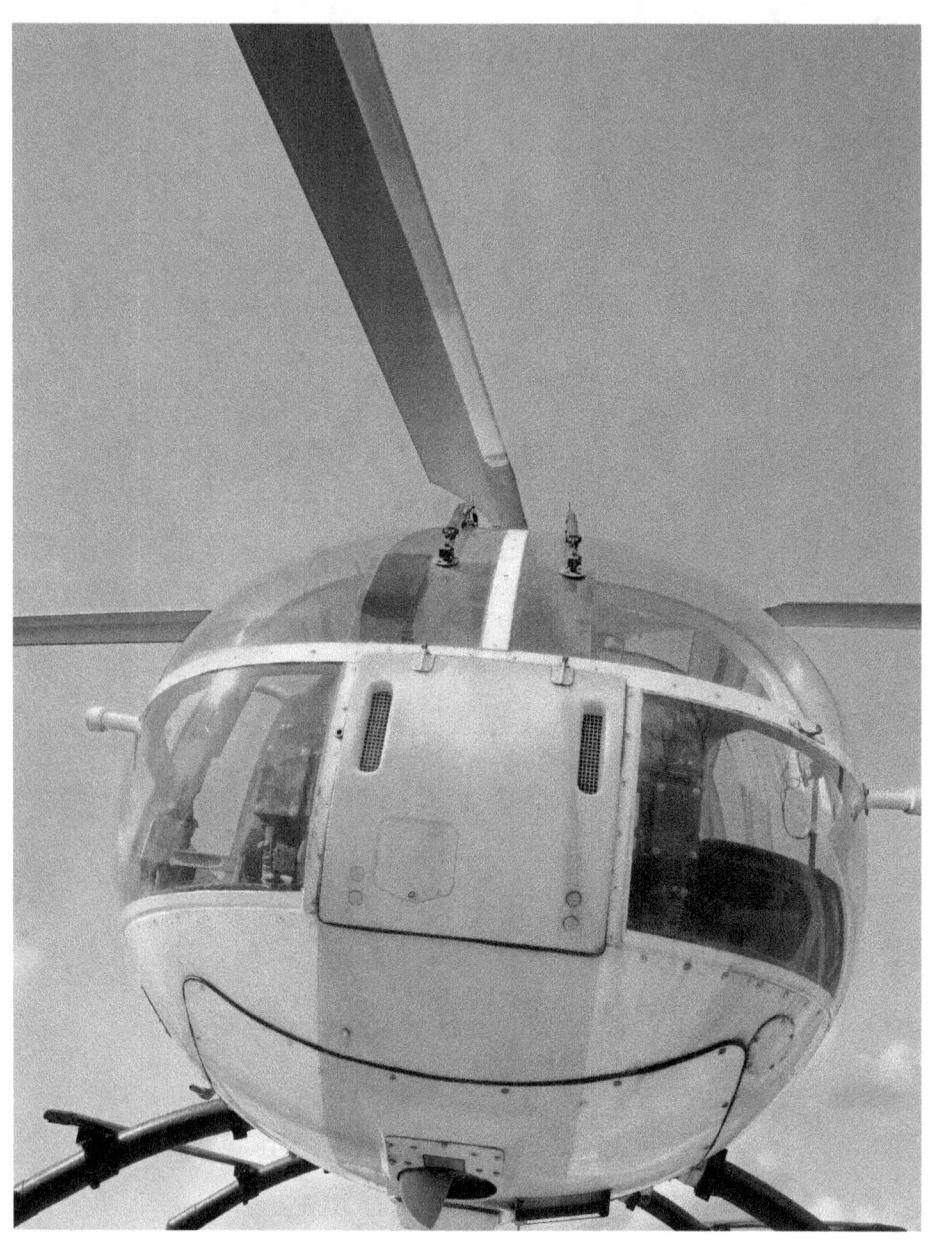

Rescue GoGo

You docked and found me
whisked me off aways

out to sea and cold waters
gone for days

the engine blew and we drifted
more days

then along came a big basket
in windy sea sprays

friends ashore clapped our backs
I guess they missed us

Good Mischief

Outlaw guns and Viagra
from Hong Kong to the Saharra

Archive "sacred" texts
Sodom and Gomorrah

No more golf or fishing
bastions and Begorrah

The good it'll do!
real law and order

Lodging with Mountain Views

Driver and co-pilot, we
Along infinite highways, we go
and downtown mazes, through

The children's graduations
from "higher learning," that is
a key quest completed, that is why

We two go, to the ceremony whereupon
the institution stamps, when the children get
words for tender resumes, that is why

College town hotels, out of the question
we booked an off-road solution
climbed rough terrains, up
into the mountains, up and around, to
a one-night home, a majestic domain
whereupon
a mountaintop goddess and her dog
guarded our sleep at the top of the world,
a scenic picture window as headboard

Awakened, refreshed, we hastened
and rose to the occasion

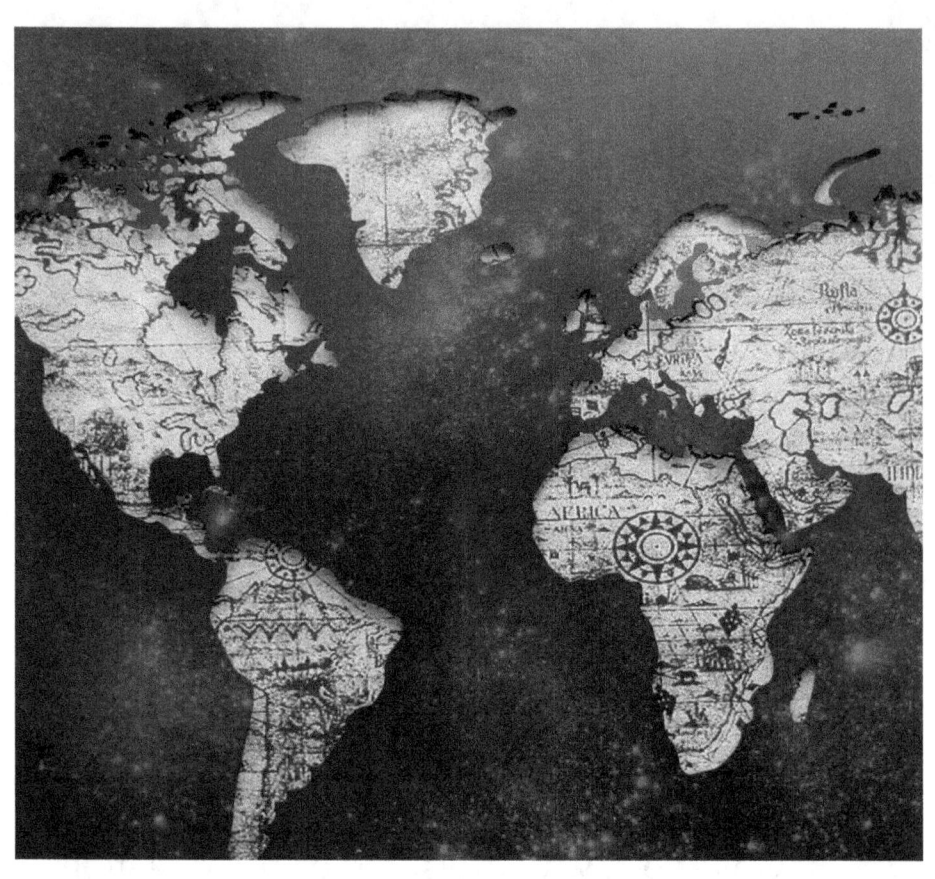

Are Men Too Emotional To Lead?

There's more than enough blame to go around
From the Arctic Circle to way down south

From Hong Kong to the Congo, Brussels, Berlin
Who among us has n'er sinned?

Madrid, Milan, London, Paris
People may be bad but we look marvelous

From New York to Dubai, London, Beijing
Thems with the gold get all the bling

Tel Aviv to Beirut, Moscow and Honah Lee
Blood fights and bromance, fellas puh-lease

Enough is enough! Let the women take charge
Move out of the way, go play in the garage

How To Write A Poem In Five Easy Steps

1) Start with a tiny idea
a glimmer of magic
a funny list
a random object
a beautiful bird
a catchy word
a whole line
a nice rhyme

2) set it free
jot it down
ideas are fickle
and liable to flee

3) Follow your heart
there's a good start
mere amusement!
then pull it taut

4) That's more or less it

5) Oh, and less is more

Wanted: Enlightened Witness

A radically new perspective
away from the cult
out of jeopardy
a lightening bolt

An enlightened witness
a power reader
with mortal fitness
an extraordinary healer

Someone to hear the story
is what you need
Justice and Glory
Godspeed

A Great Honor

I accept the verdict
as they decree
their silly ban
has me in good company

At every turn
every fork in the road
the decisions were mine
and mine alone

Oh! I ceded some
and vetoed more
the territory that's mine
I'll defend and hold

I really must say
how delighted I am
to be here writing
to you today

I've Got It All Figured Out

Well almost...

Every time I get close
they move the ends
but I'll catch on someday
you can depend

The other trouble is
I'm losing money
minding my biz
the math is funny

Well I plant my flag!
to defend this hill
if I can't do it now
I probably never will

About NG Swett

The writer lives on an island in the Outer Lands Archipelago off the US East Coast.

Acknowledgements

Thank You for reading this collection of poems. Something magical happens when a piece of writing is read. As a reader, you're completing a circle of life, word by word.

Thank you **Mom and Dad** for passing down the gifts of literature and art and for your courageous and passionate examples.

Thank you to my late **grandmother, Nancy B. Stalker,** for being the most constant and loving pen pal anyone could ask for.

Thank you to the person to whom this collection is dedicated, **CW Swett,** my spouse, for a lifetime of love, encouragement, tireless patience, a wealth of life experiences I couldn't have had without you, and your generous support.

Thank you to our two **grown children** just for being born and shining your beautiful, loving lights on the world. My top fans!!

This lady lit the way to making books and guided me on my path with encouragement and all the tools and options: the amazing **Cyndi Zlotow**. Thank you, Cyndi!

Last but not least, I thank the many **beta readers, friends, teachers, relatives, fellow creatives, subscribers and other individuals** who made this collection possible by reading, sharing their knowledge, encouragement, and invaluable feedback.

About 4seasonshelf

You're invited to connect with NG Swett and 4seasonshelf!

Go to www.4seasonshelf.com, join the list, and connect on social media.

www.4seasonshelf.com

www.ingramcontent.com/pod-product-compliance
Lightning Source LLC
Chambersburg PA
CBHW050335010526
44119CB00004B/155